YOUR KNOWLEDGE HAS VALUE

Bibliographic information published by the German National Library:

The German National Library lists this publication in the National Bibliography; detailed bibliographic data are available on the Internet at http://dnb.dnb.de .

Imprint:

Copyright © 2014 GRIN Verlag, Open Publishing GmbH
Print and binding: Books on Demand GmbH, Norderstedt Germany
ISBN: 978-3-656-96353-0

This book at GRIN:

http://www.grin.com/en/e-book/300046/the-impact-of-effective-teaching-strategies-on-the-students-academic-performance

Laraib Nasir Jalbani

The Impact of Effective Teaching Strategies on the Students' Academic Performance and Learning Outcome

A Literature Review

GRIN Publishing

GRIN - Your knowledge has value

Since its foundation in 1998, GRIN has specialized in publishing academic texts by students, college teachers and other academics as e-book and printed book. The website www.grin.com is an ideal platform for presenting term papers, final papers, scientific essays, dissertations and specialist books.

Visit us on the internet:

http://www.grin.com/

http://www.facebook.com/grincom

http://www.twitter.com/grin_com

IMPACT OF EFFECTIVE TEACHING STRATEGIES ON STUDENTS' ACADEMIC PERFORMACE AND LEARNING OUTCOME: A LITERATURE REVIEW

Laraib Nasir Jalbani

Department of Education

College of Economics and Social Development

Institute of Business Management

August 2014

Abstract

This discussion focuses on impact of effective teaching strategies on the students' academic performance and learning outcome along with the researcher's own experiences. A teacher plays a vital role within a few hours in the classroom by delivering the daily specific planned content which is a part of curriculum for a specific grade. It depends on the teacher to plan it out and use effective strategies for its instructional deliverance. Teachers must have passion for learning and teaching as well as to understand needs and interests of the students. World is changing and advancing day by day, so teachers need to be technology savvies as well, in order to meet new global emerging demands.

Introduction

Stakeholders all over the world strive for quality education of children. First of all, there is a need to define quality education so that one can differentiate it from less-preferred education. Similarly, there are many educators and researchers who have debated that there are some school variables which influence the students' achievement in particular. According to Coleman (2003), minimal role is played by the schools as far as the students' achievement is concerned because it is independent of their background as well as societal factors. On the other hand, a few researchers suggest that factors like class size and space (Glass 2001), the teachers' qualification (Ferguson, 2004), the school's size and space (Haller, 1993), and a few more variables play a vital role in what the students learn in general.

Explaining Quality Teaching

Research points out that Quality teaching is tend to necessarily be student-centred. It aims to help most and for all students learning. Therefore, focus should not only be pedagogical skills, but also learning environment that must address the students' personal needs. Students should also be aware as to why they are working so that they are able to relate to other students and receive help if required.

As a result, great emphasis has been laid on "quality teaching" by many educators. In the same way, there is a need of elaborating the term "quality teaching". Globalization has influenced each and everyone's life. Quality, successful and effective learning actually depends on several factors e.g. availability and selection of instructional resources, staffing quality, nature and its level, professional development implication as a system, and also the support of parents and administration. Recently, research also highlights one of the key features of "quality teaching" i.e. student-centred classrooms, which aims to benefit all students learning.

Global demands and changes

Therefore, learning environment along with teachers' pedagogical skills is important for quality education (Johnson, 2007). Similarly, the students have also become both, geographically and socially diversified. There is a great need of new teaching methods and pedagogies to meet global challenges. Hence, we can say that there is also a need of change in the learner and teachers' means of interaction. All the schools are striving to integrate curriculum with technology so that the students are provided quality education and learning takes place their way and they are focusing to provide quality education to the students by all the means so that they are ahead in the education industry.

Aiding to Growth

According to Alton-Lee (2004), the teachers should align their professional experiences with their teaching practices and pedagogies in order to benefit their students. Agreeing to Alton-Lee, these days one of the major roles of the teachers is to ensure that the content delivered has achieved the learning objective, which can be considered a key challenge. Despite the years of teaching experience, there is always a room for improvement and innovation for the teachers to adapt as per their requirement. Demands and needs change time to time so the teachers should also undergo professional and personal development to benefit both, the students and themselves as well, both are the learners. There is no age limit for learning; it depends on priorities and awareness only.

Reflective inquiry

Another researcher, Deppeler (2000), suggests that the teachers would be able to change their teaching practices when they would reflect upon them and engage themselves in examining their own theories of teaching practices. But, ironically, it is a fact that the teachers hardly get any time to reflect on their daily practices, leading to improvement, or they are unaware of this process and it is out of question for them. They believe that delivering the content which has been planned for a specific day and subject is the basic necessity, neglecting the fact and being least bothered about knowing if the student learned or it was impossible for a student to grasp the basic concept even.

Effective variables

Roshenshine and Furst have introduced five variables of a teacher's effectiveness, these are Variability, Clarity, Task-oriented, Enthusiasm and the last one is the students' opportunity to learn criterion material. We must say that these are indeed a few components essential for a teacher to be known as effective, but there are more key elements which help the teachers personally and professionally and also their students. These are being reflective, empathizing when required, respect students, a good communicator, her/his own love of learning and many more which makes a teacher effective and the most important part is the instruction strategy which he/she chooses to deliver content which helps students in learning more effectively.

Content (What) and Strategy (How)

Most of the teachers think that they can improve their teaching practices through developing sound knowledge of content that needs to be taught and delivered (Hill and Crevola, 2003). This is a major drawback in many schools. The teachers lose focus on their teaching strategies and they assume that the learners face difficulties because the content (**what** needs to be taught and delivered) is complicated or not of their interest, instead of realizing the fact that the teaching strategy (**how** to teach and deliver) should be more effective and as per their requirement and needs in order to generate their interest and better learning opportunity for the students. Furthermore, both, **how** and **what** are linked together but still far different and unique in nature.

Unique individual with unique learning style

All the educationists are well familiar with the fact that all the learners have a different learning style, whereas the problem lies in catering to all of them with an effective teaching strategy. Students learn in different ways as per their capabilities. Some learn by seeing, hearing, reflecting, modelling, reasoning, and drawing etc (Felder, 1998). With an agreement to Felder, similarly there are different teaching styles as well. Some give lectures, some discuss the topic, some make their students work in groups, some use technology, some use textbooks and many more. But, the main purpose behind these efforts is to help students grasp content knowledge and align them with the real world scenario.

Teaching strategies and age groups

Teaching strategies vary from one age group to another. None of the method is the best. It depends on the learning style of students. Primary students take more interest in the activities performed in the class. In-class exercises work the best for this age group. Visual and auditory aids improve learning and performance. Whereas, for secondary and tertiary levels, lectures, projects, field work, group exercises and peer teaching are the most suitable strategies to help them. Howard Gardner's multiple intelligences are also being considered and integrated in the lesson plans for improved learning of each and every student.

Reflecting on experiences

I have always taught primary classes so my experience cannot be considered diverse. However, I, along with the other teachers of the same level have tried to integrate teaching strategies which would help students in the best possible way. My teaching strategies were lectures, some kinaesthetic activities like role play, assignments, short reflections, pictorial PowerPoint slides, verbal discussions etc. On the other hand, the students enjoyed the most when they were taken to the computer lab or exposed to nature, especially for science.

Conclusion

Great emphasis has been laid on the teachers to use effective teaching strategies and method for improved learning by many researchers and educationists but on the other hand, one must also understand that the amount of students' learning in a class also depends on their native ability of cognition and as well as their prior preparation. Teachers should prepare mental set through rapport with students before they start teaching. With the passage of time, the importance of instructors' teaching style is being spread and the teachers are taking initiative to improve their teaching strategies for students' improved learning by getting enrolled in such programmes which help them reflect upon their teaching practices and improving them as per requirement. The teachers who are willing for professional development in this area are able to deliver even complex and complicated content effectively, helping the students generate their interest and eagerness for more opportunities of learning in a conducive environment, making all the individuals feel that they are being taught in their own unique way being unique themselves.

Bibliography

Barbe, WB., R.H. Swassing and M.N. Milone (1995). *Teaching Through Modality Strengths: Concepts and Practices,* Zaner-Bloser, Columbus, Ohio.

Darling-Hammond, L. (2000). *Teacher quality and student achievement*: A review of state policy evidence. *Education Policy Analysis Archives, 8*(1).

Hill, P., Crévola, C., & Hopkins, D. (2010). *Teaching and Learning as the Heartland of School Improvement. IARTV Seminar Series.* December. No. 100. Melbourne.

Marzano, R. J., Pickering, D. J., & Pollock, J. E. (2007). *Classroom instruction that works: Research-based strategies for increasing student achievement.* Alexandria, VA: Association for Supervision and Curriculum Development

Rosenshine, B., & Furst, N. (1973). *Research on teacher performance criteria.* In B.O. Smith (Ed.), *Research in teacher education: A symposium.* Englewood Cliffs, NJ: Prentice-Hall.

Thousand, J., & Villa, R., & Nevin, A. (2007). *Differentiated Instruction: Collaborative Planning & Teaching for Universally Designed Lessons.* California: Corwin Press (800) 818-7423.

Walls, R.T., & Cather, W.L. (2003). *Principles of instruction.* Emittsburg, MD: National Emergency Training Center.

Walls, R.T. (1996). *Concepts of learning: 99 truths.* In Federal Emergency Management Agency (Ed.), *Instructor one.* Emmitsburg, MD: National Emergency Training Center.

Wright, S. P., Horn, S. P., & Sanders, W. L. (1997). *Teacher and classroom context effects on student achievement: Implications for teacher evaluation. Journal of Personnel Evaluation in Education, 11*, 57–67, p. 63